Woody is out riding,
when his **hat** flies off his head!
"Oh no! **That hat** looks **bad**!"
says Jessie.

Woody's New Hat

ISBN: 978-1-338-57284-1

10 9 8 7 6 5 4 3 2 1   19 20 21 22 23

Printed in Malaysia   106

First printing, 2019

Book design by Marissa Asuncion

Scholastic Inc.

Jessie **has** a lot of **hats**.
"You **can** take your pick,"
says Jessie.

Woody puts on a brown **hat**.
"This **hat** is too big,"
says Woody.

Woody put on a yellow **hat**.
"This **hat** is too **fancy**,"
says Woody.

Jessie **has** a lot of **hats**.
She **has** red **hats** and blue **hats**.
But, she **has** no **hat** for Woody.

Woody is **sad**.
He does not **have** a **hat**.

"All I want is a brown **hat**
with a big brim" he says.

Woody's horse **has** a **plan**.
He **grabs** a **hat**.

It is a brown **hat**.
It **has** a big brim.

Look **at that**!
It is Woody's old **hat**!
It does not look so **bad**.

Woody is **glad**.
He **has** his
old brown **hat back**.